THE WORLD ON OUR STREET

By

Gail-Ann Brown

Copyright @2020 by Gail Ann Brown

A rights reserved. No part of this publication may be reproduced, stored in a retrieval system, or transmitted in any form or by any means electronic, mechanical, photocopying, recording, or otherwise without the written permission of the authors.

Limits of Liability-Disclaimer

The authors and publisher shall not be liable for your misuse of this material. The purpose of this book is to educate and empower. The authors and/or publisher do not guarantee that anyone following these techniques, suggestions, tips, ideas, and/or strategies will become successful.

The authors and/or publisher shall have neither liability nor responsibility to anyone with respect to any loss or damage caused or alleged to be caused directly or indirectly by the information contained in this book.

DEDICATION

I would love to dedicate this book to my son and daughter. May you forever love learning and keep your love for adventure.

Jordan and Ava loved summertime. It was the time of year that the whole family usually went on an adventure, sometimes traveling to faraway places. "Mama what are we doing for summer vacation this year?" asked Jordan.
"Are we going on a plane again?" asked Ava.

School just got out for summer vacation and Jordan and Ava were eager to know the Family's summer plans.

"Well kids, " This year we will be doing something a bit different, we're having a staycation."
"A staycation? What's that?" Ava asked.
" What do you do on a staycation?" Jordan asked.

At dinner that evening Jordan was still not happy about the idea of a staycation.
"Dad, Mom says we're doing a staycation this summer it sounds boring. There's nothing to do but stay home," Jordan sighed as he expressed how he disliked the idea.

"Well Jordan, sometimes things have to change, and we can find new ways of doing things." Dad explained. "I'm sure you and Ava will have fun on our staycation, Mom and I have made some plans I know you will enjoy."

"What will we do first?" Ava asked.
"First we'll have a potluck," Mom explained.
"What's a potluck?" Jordan asked.
"Well, it's a dinner where friends come over and they bring their favorite dish," Mom explained.

"That means we can try different kinds of food that our neighbors bring," Dad said. "That sounds yummy." Jordan said.
"There will be lots of food!" Ava shouted, everyone laughed.

On the day of the potluck Jordan and Ava helped their Mom and Dad, get the house ready for all their guests.

They baked their favorite cookies with Mom and helped to set the table. Dad made his famous barbeque on the grill, everything smelled so good.

"We have a surprise for you," said Mom.
"What is it?" asked Jordan.
"Everyone coming to the Potluck will dress up in their native dress", Mom said.
"What is native dress?" asked Ava.
"It is the style of dress from the country where you were born", Dad said.

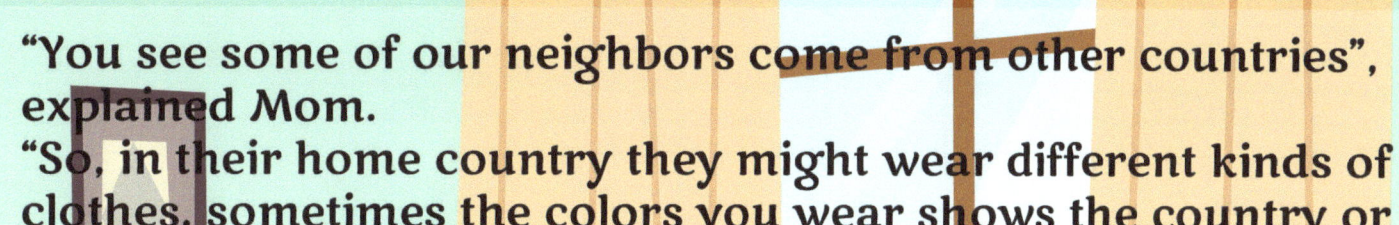

"You see some of our neighbors come from other countries", explained Mom.
"So, in their home country they might wear different kinds of clothes, sometimes the colors you wear shows the country or area you come from".
"So, what are we going wear"? Jordan asked.

"Yes, you do, in fact Grandma made a dress especially for you", Dad said.
"Awesome"! Ava shouted.

Soon everyone was dressed and ready to welcome their guest. Ava loved her dress and twirled around the living room. Jordan felt special in his Jamaican tropical shirt.

Soon the time came for the guests to arrive and the family worked together to set out the food they prepared.

The doorbell rang and Jordan shouted, "They're here".
Dad opened the door.

It was a wonderful sight to see neighbors that lived on their street dressed in many different colorful outfits.

Parents and kids wore matching outfits like Jordan and Ava and their parents. Right here in their house were people from all over the world, and they brought a dish from their home country.

Everyone went on the patio and put out the food on the buffet for all to enjoy. Everything smelled delicious.
"Can we eat now?", asked Jordan.

The potluck was a big success everyone had a great time trying new foods and talking about the country they came from.

Soon it was time for bed. Mom and Dad came to tuck Jordan and Ava in bed.

"I learned a lot too", Jordan said, "Did you know we have neighbors from Liberia, Sweden, China, Columbia and New Zealand?"

"Wow that's a lot of places" Mom said.

"Mom, Dad, we have the world on our street"! Shouted Jordan. They all laughed.

ABOUT THE AUTHOR

I am Gail-Ann Brown, a wife, mother, and educator who loves to travel and explore new cultures. As a lover of the great outdoors, a beach baby, and an adventurist, this passion was ignited in me by my parents who took me on summer adventures throughout my childhood. I have tried to instill my passion in my children and hope to do the same through my books.

The world is an exciting and interesting place. Getting to know our neighbors at home and abroad makes our world even more interesting. Embracing other cultures adds interest to our world and helps us to see all the beauties that it holds.

contact g-ambrown@hotmail.com

www.ingramcontent.com/pod-product-compliance
Lightning Source LLC
Chambersburg PA
CBHW060800090426
42736CB00002B/98